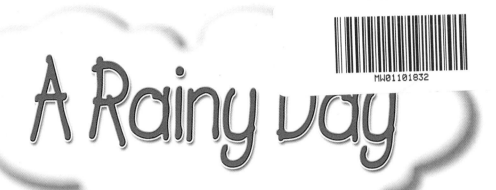

A Rainy Day

By Donna Latham

Illustrated by Aleksey Ivanov

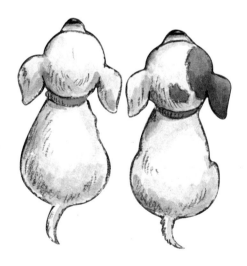

Target Skill Consonant Ll /l/

PEARSON

Scott Foresman

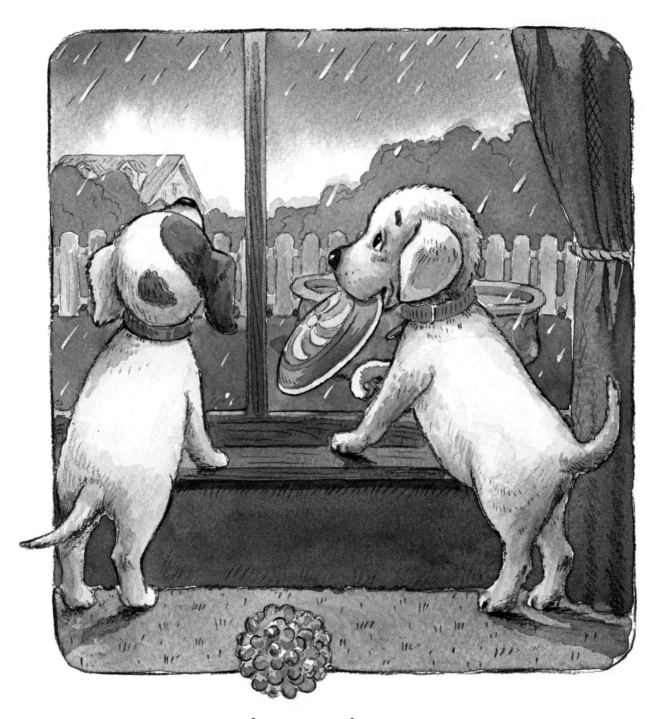

Look at that, Lin!

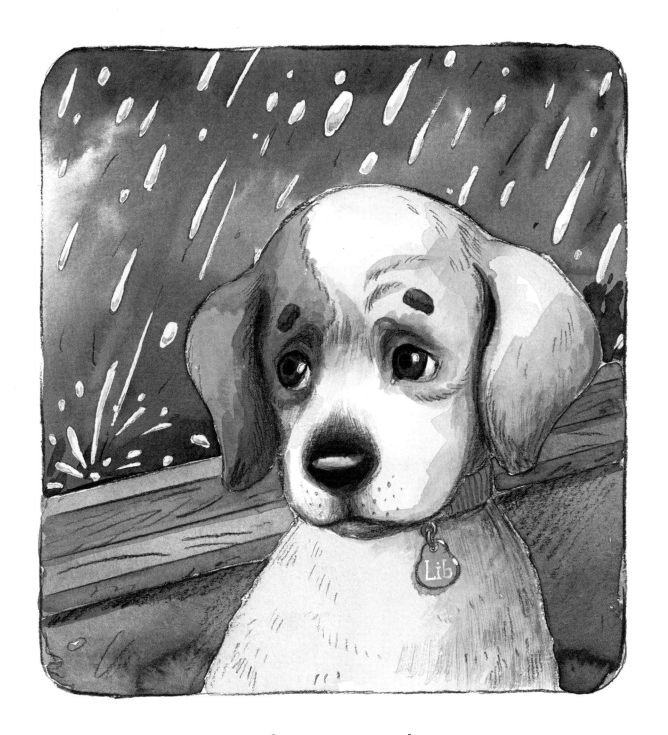

Lib is sad.

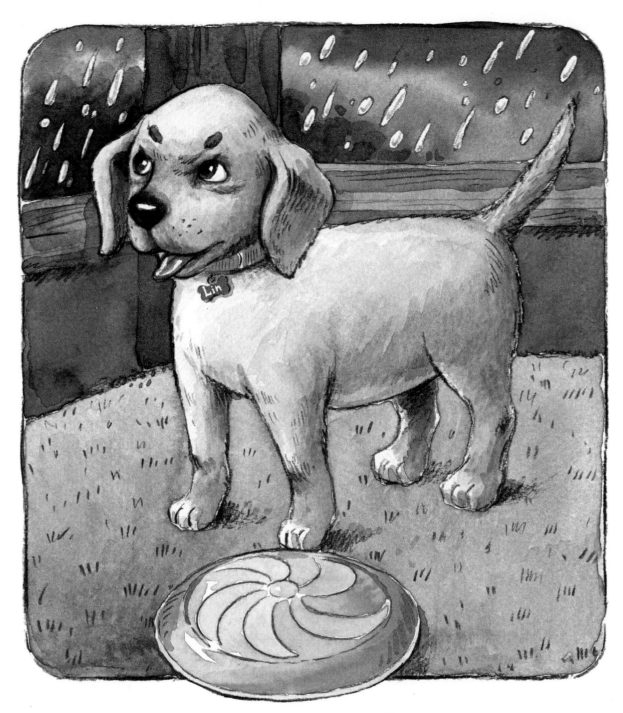

Lin is mad.

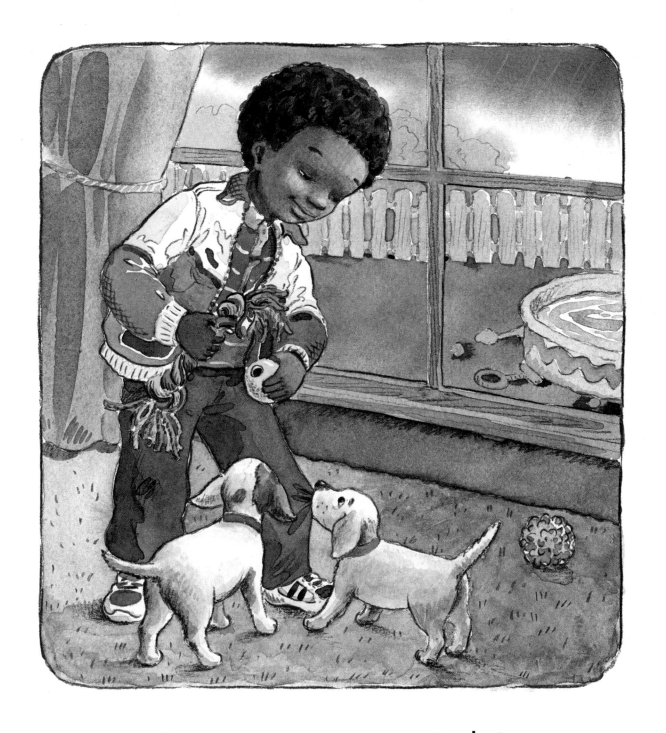

Do you see it, Rob?

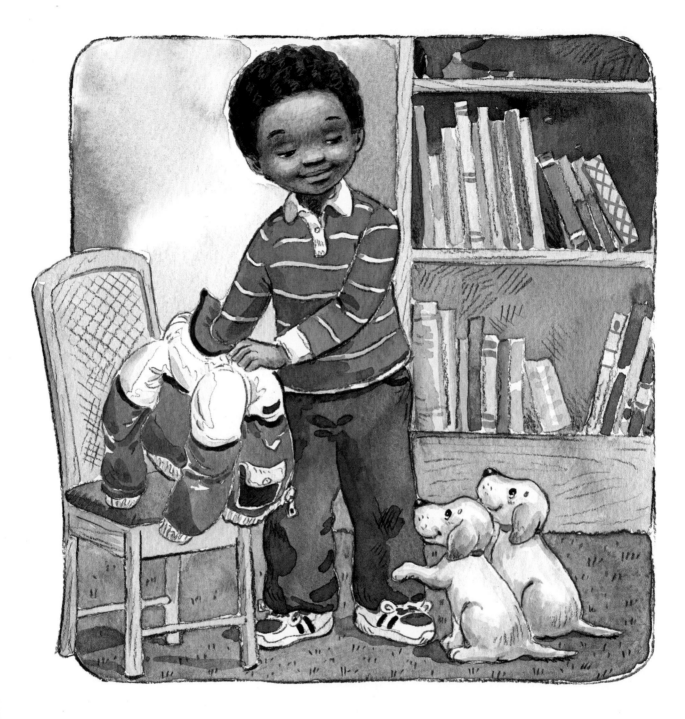

Are you sad, Rob?

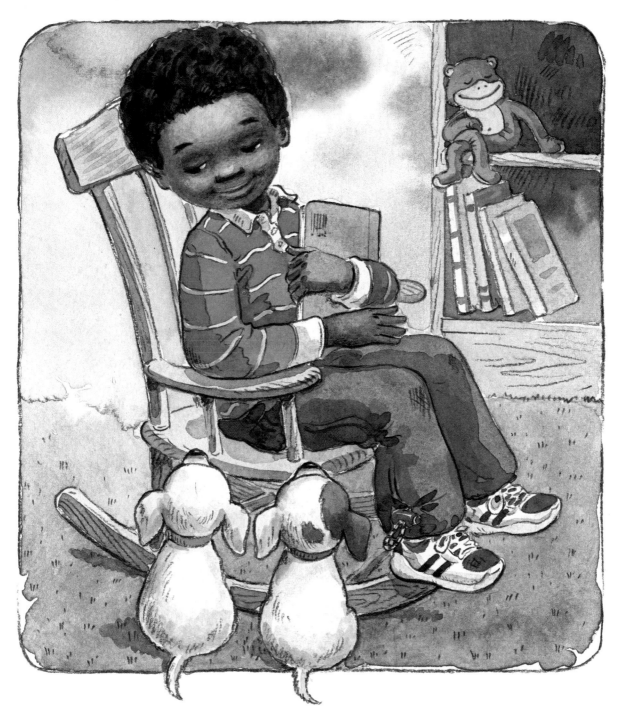

Hop on my lap.

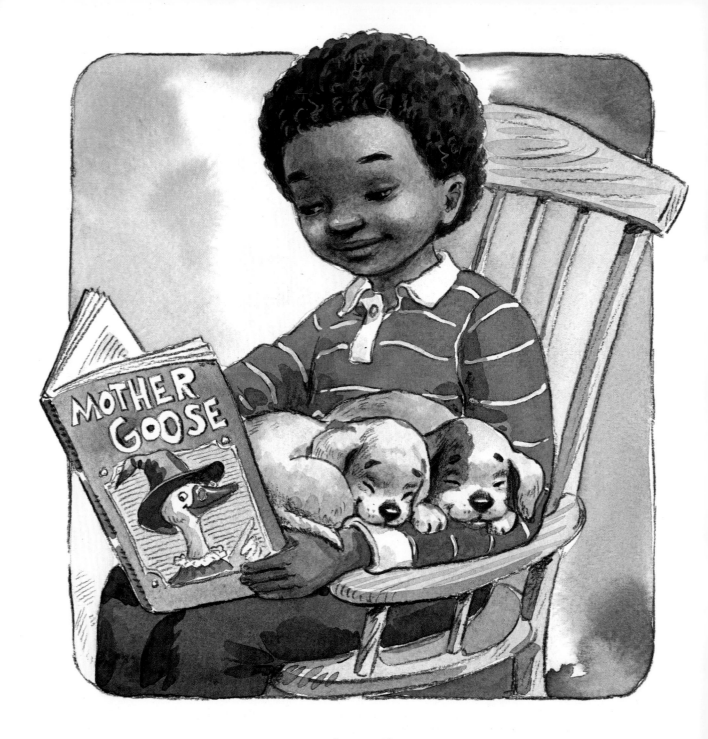

Lin and Lib nap!